6/11

D0539805

East Sussex Library and
Information Services

East Sussex
County Council

POLEGATE LIBRARY
WINDSOR WAY,
POLEGATE, BN26 6QF
Renewals Tel: 0345 60 80 195
Enquiries Tel: 0345 60 80 196
Please return/renew this item by the last
date shown.
Books may also be renewed by phone or
internet.
www.eastsussex.gov.uk/libraries

HUGO WILLIAMS

Dear Room

ff

faber and faber

First published in 2006
by Faber and Faber Limited
3 Queen Square London WC1N 3AU

Photoset by RefineCatch Limited, Bungay, Suffolk
Printed in England by T.J. International Ltd, Padstow, Cornwall

Some of these poems have appeared in *Poetry Review, London Magazine,
London Review of Books, Acumen, Rising, Leviathan, Tatler, The New
Review, Guardian, The Printer's Devil, Times Literary Supplement,
Independent on Sunday.*

A CIP record for this book is available from the British Library

ISBN 978-0-571-23037-2
0-571-23037-7

2 4 6 8 10 9 7 5 3 1

Contents

DEAR ROOM

Outline

There used to be a door here.
You could walk straight in off the street.
Look, there's the old footscraper
someone's forgotten to take away.
This must be the doorstep
where I waited so patiently.

It's all bricked up now.
You have to go round by the porter's lodge.
But if you look carefully
you can still see the outline of the door.
You can still make out
where the entryphone used to be.

Dear Room

Are you still Chinese yellow?
Are your blinds still drawn
against prying eyes on the tops of buses?
How well I remember you
perched beside a traffic light
on the corner of Ladbroke Grove,
our tree-house lookout post,
shuddering and shaking all night
to the jamming of gears,
the headlights of cars
kerb-crawling the platform where we slept.
You held us suspended
half-way between heaven and hell.
We climbed up into the fork
of our lookout tree
and kicked the ladder away.

*

You were more a part of the street
than part of the house,
which only seemed to exist
as a doorway, a darkened hall,
an excited flight of stairs.

You were a half-floor,
tacked to the side of the building
as an afterthought, an extension of the landing
suspended in mid-air.
We tried not to walk too heavily.

Room, you taught us to live dangerously,
striped light coming through the blinds
and falling on the bed
where we lay too close to the edge.
Love in that half-world

was a seabird's egg, tapered and weighted
to roll only in that circle
which the ledge allowed was tenable.
If one of us lost balance
we would tumble into the street.

*

I've heard she keeps you on
as a studio, somewhere to escape to
from new-found domesticity.
Once or twice a week – or is it less? –
she'll drop by to water the plants, sulk,

or do a little work
sorting through her old stuff for jumble sale.
I think of her, getting ready to go out,
meeting my gaze in the long mirror,
eyes already sheeted for departure.

Room, you must be wondering
what she is planning to do with you
now that everything is stripped bare, made good,
painted matt magnolia.
I've been wondering the same thing myself.

As she picks up an old blue dress
and holds it against herself for a moment,
I almost imagine her
staring at me across London,
daring me to blink.

Helter-Skelter

We go back a long way, you and I,
on the bumper cars
and the Golden Galloper
to a helter-skelter
spiralling out of the water
on Brighton's Palace Pier.

You wanted to go on it
'because it was there',
so we took our mat
and climbed the rickety ladder
to a sort of platform
above the clouds.

We went down together
in a whirl of blue sky
and white stucco,
calling each other's name
and holding our hands in the air.
It was all over in a flash.

We hardly had time
to feel happy, then sad,
when we shot round a corner
and came to a rest where we are,
still clinging together
in a tangle of arms and legs.

Horse and Dolphin Yard

We go back even further than that,
down Macclesfield Street
into Horse and Dolphin Yard.
I pushed you ahead of me
over rain-greased cobblestones,
looking for somewhere quiet to be alone.
We had stumbled into a scene
out of Old Kowloon,
pig carcasses hanging up,
bug-infested neon, a Chinese cook
who stopped sharpening his knife
and turned to look at us.
Fetid, tropical air from an extractor fan
mixed with the smell of your hair.

Party Tricks

A drop of something cloudy blue
hangs between two grave, attentive breasts,
which sway back and forth
like cobras under a cloth.
Her nipples flicker on and off
in amused disbelief
as I do the Indian rope trick
with my gin and tonic.

The liquid dawdles for a moment in mid-air,
then changes its mind
and comes down gradually
all over her top half.
Her nipples give me ten out of ten
as I write my name and telephone number
on a damp paper napkin
and take up smoking again.

Tell

To find out if she really likes you,
drop something at her feet. As you bend to pick it up,
glance upwards. If she's looking down at you
and meets your eye, it means she likes you.
If she's taking advantage of the moment
to check out the room, prepare for a bumpy ride.

Her Argument

She presents her argument
in three more or less equal parts –
cotton, leather and bare skin,

each one cross-referenced
with the other two, in what looks like
a watertight case.

Please Come Late

Please come late,
so that I have almost given you up
and have started glancing round the room,
thinking everyone is you.
Please don't come
until I have started missing you,
thinking I will never see you again,
praying you still exist.
Come too late for forgiveness.
Make me suffer
wondering what you are doing
still in your dressing gown
on the other side of town.
Make me beg for mercy
when you pick up a magazine.

Are you looking in your mirror,
suddenly remembering me?
I'm on my second coffee by now,
eating the little bits of sugar in my cup.
Haven't you even set out yet?
I decide I don't want to see you after all.
I don't really like you.
I'd rather be on my own.
I know it is all over between us,
but I go on sitting here,
reading a newspaper,
not understanding a word.
If you came in now I wouldn't recognise you.
Don't come anywhere near me
until I have gone slightly mad for love of you.

Come On Up

I thought about you as crudely as possible,
till my hand reached for the phone
and I heard you laughing
on the other end of the line.

I'll never forget your rejection of my plan
to see a film at the weekend.
'I can't think that far ahead,' you explained.
'What are you doing right now?'

I wasn't doing anything of course.
I remember your voice on the entryphone:
'Come on up, Sunny Jim!'
I took the stairs two at a time.

Archaeology

The damaged hieroglyph
of a man on a horse
was easily settled
when he went to her house,

but the crossed key
she holds in her left hand
is a symbol of likelihood
we cannot establish.

Sighs

Her skill with angles, signals, orders, murmurs, sighs,
as if a great ship were getting under way,
its coloured streamers lifting and breaking finally
as it pulled away from the quay.

Pillow Talk

It was a big boat, big at the back,
with plenty of room at the side.
The nursery was three floors up, overlooking the pool.
They had a ceremony for dunking people in it
who hadn't been across the equator.
I didn't mind, but one little boy started crying
because he thought they were killing his mother,
so we had to go up to the nursery
and watch from there, but we couldn't see properly.
Patty was particularly furious about this
because we were both interested in people drowning.

We used to get off the boat occasionally
and do things like going down a gold mine
or to a carpet museum.
Once we stopped at a place where all the black people
were selling red juice and calling out.
Daddy insisted on trying some
and reported back that it was only beetroot.
It was brilliant when we went on the horse and cart
because it was really steep going up
and the horse kept stumbling and foaming at the mouth.
I was excited because I thought we were going to
fall over the cliff. Then we went to a convent
and had lime juice on a big lawn,
which we loved, fresh.

Our mother was having lessons in making
Chinese pictures of birds,
which my father said was a complete waste of time.
A friend of his had disappeared in British North Borneo.

Patty and I used to go around pretending we were mad,
asking people for money.
We were given old-fashioned aprons, French,
with soft red lines,
which we had to put on for our lessons.
We were going somewhere like Fiji or Mauritius,
but first we had to go to British North Borneo.

In Yokohama our teacher came on board
in full ceremonial costume, then,
after he had told us about Japan,
he sat on the floor and demonstrated hari kiri.
You put your sword in here
and move it across from left to right,
then up and down, until you die,
or your friend has to cut your head off.
Daddy was furious,
but Patty and I thoroughly enjoyed ourselves.
We loved it when the lights went out
and the Captain told everyone not to worry.

There were always two sittings for dinner,
but we always had to go to the first one.
Now what is important is that I never ate anything.
Everyone was worried stiff.
Then they discovered I was eating Chinese food
with the amah. She used to stir it with her chopsticks
and test it in her mouth,
until one day she spat it out and I thought ugh!
After that, I discovered spaghetti
and powdered mashed potato with grated cheese.

We used to hide our sausages in it
and pretend we'd lost them. Or ham.
I played with mine so much I couldn't possibly eat it.

At the end of the journey, in England, or Hong Kong,
the Chef came out of the kitchen
with his big hat on.
We were sitting at a big table
with a big white table cloth, empty,
but even though it was only a children's table
it was very beautiful. Everything was quiet.
Then the Chef lifted me up – he was huge –
and put me on the table
in the middle of this lovely white tablecloth.
He put this bright red sash on me with a big bow.
It looked completely brilliant, with gold lettering
saying 'MISS SPAGHETTI 1969'.

The Crazy Room

Stiffened velvet drapes hung upwards.
Carpets, furniture, a pair of embroidered
Turkish slippers had been fastened to
the ceiling. A stuffed dog lay in a basket
looking down at me, while an elaborate
chandelier thrust upwards from the floor.
I laughed at the crazy room, until I saw
the candles burning downwards.

Pieces of Sky

Pieces of sky ran across the ceiling,
slid down walls,
gathered in pools on the floor.
Light spilled over the furniture,
splashed up into our faces.
We cupped it in our hands,
let it run through our fingers.

It played round our ankles,
came up over our knees, our shoulders.
We were out of our depth
in the cross-currents of yellow and blue
that hauled us in and out of the days.
We were swimming through colours,
treading water for our lives.

What's Keeping Me

On the other side of the wall
you are waiting for me
to finish cleaning my teeth
and come to bed with you.
I linger in front of the mirror
while you get undressed.
Hardly the time or place
for idle contemplation, and yet,
how strange to be alive,
able to do anything I like!

Time, which had been running on
too fast, slows to a trace
of rose carnation
in the looking-glass bathroom
where your likeness flickers, beckons,
puts out its tongue at me.
I find myself practising
your 'No' face in the mirror,
while you stretch and yawn
and put on moisturiser.

What was it your mother told you
that so excited me?
'Wash your hands and get on with it.'
What's keeping me then?
I lean on the taps and stare.
On the other side of the wall
you are completely naked by now,
bending over, sweeping the crumbs
from the naughty white sheet
that wants to go to bed with you.

In Your Sleep

When you fall asleep tonight
and you twist and turn
and throw the covers back,
I can look at your arms and neck,
I can look at your face if I want to.
I can look as long as I like,
so long as I don't wake you.

When you turn to me in your sleep
and your mouth opens
and you put one arm round my neck,
I can lay my hand on your hip,
I can touch your breast if I want to.
I can do whatever I like,
so long as I don't hurt you.

Ink

I have gone over my loved one's face
in ink, for something to do.
I wanted to see how she looked
telling me not to.
I traced a well-worn path
back and forth between her eyes
in search of crumbs.
I ran the gauntlet of her tantrums.

I gave her horn-rimmed spectacles,
blacking them in
where her eyes accused me
of following her round the room.
I joined up her eyes and mouth
in a rough-hewn triangle, a monkey face.
Wasn't I her pet?
Her little marmoset?

I went through the paper
and the paper beneath,
crossing out her kindness to the dog.
My pen snagged the corner of her mouth,
spattering ink on my cuff.
Jagged lines shot this way and that,
tearing her skin
as I scribbled my gaze on her.

Playing Safe

I liked not liking you too much.
I liked playing safe. Not being bowled over by you
was part of the thrill.
At the King's Palace Hotel
you couldn't take your hands off me,
you couldn't care less
how quickly or stupidly we made love,
so long as it happened.
So why should it ever end?

I never dreamed you were serious
when you put me on probation
for 'loitering without intent'.
We could still talk from time to time, you said,
but we weren't going out any more,
was that understood?
If only you didn't still love me
I'd be all right. I could think about you calmly,
without crying, or writing letters.

The Words

Hearing the words for the first time
I come back feebly
with a plea for clemency:
'I can't believe I'm never going to
sleep with you again.'

Horrible to hear such things
coming out of my mouth
at a time like this,
but she is generous in victory:
'You know we will,' she tells me seriously.

'But when?' I ask,
blowing all hope of recovery.
'When you're not expecting it,' she replies.
How can I convince her
that I'm not expecting it now?

Black Border

How long did it take you, I wonder,
to ink in the border
of your last letter?
Cross-hatched curtains
drawn back on cords
reveal a winding road
leading to 'THE END'.
A sun, worn thin with scribbling,
is going down on the scene.

Gothic illuminations,
heavy underlinings in red,
make sure I get the message
loud and clear
that there's going to be
no backsliding this time.
I hear what you're saying.
I can't help noticing
the loving care you've taken with all this.

Artist

She's working on a 'found bed',
a door panel or workbench,
bound with material like an ironing board.
She runs her hand over
its virgin flatness: not a ripple
disturbs the surface of the sheet
where the bridal couple
have been tucked to extinction.
She stands back in satisfaction,
shivering slightly in the unheated studio.

Old suitcases and games,
wardrobes and window frames
crowd round the narrow bed
teetering on its tripod.
She'll be out again tonight,
cruising the skips with her shopping trolley.
Every day the piles of junk grow higher,
the floor space smaller.
Her long-term project is a studio piece
whose completion requires her absence.

The Feast

We sit bolt upright at the banqueting table.
Our arms lie along our knees. Our high-backed chairs
have been carved with the date of our birth
and today's date. A slave brings food
made out of earth and blood. Worms crawl in it.

Dancers enter and perform our funeral rites.
Suddenly our host grows tired of the entertainment
and sends us home with gifts to mark the occasion.
We go to bed gratefully, almost weeping with relief,
only to be woken by a knock on the door.

Walk Out to Winter

Are we dead, do you think? I thought we were
when I visited your art-school annexe
and saw your things all over the floor.
Someone had nailed a dress to a board
and thrown a pot of paint at it.
We left the flowers on your desk
and went for a walk near the reservoir.

The different sets of broken promises
lay in wait for us on the muddy path.
Alibis dragged themselves out of the mire.
What was I really doing last Friday?
Why didn't you leave a message about today?
Water hovered on the brink of ice
like an eye suddenly clouding over.

I remembered a book I had read once
which tells you what to do after you die:
stay calm, accept what has happened.
Then we went for a coffee in the Union Bar
and talked about our life together.
I watched from a great distance
as you lifted the cup to your lips.

No Chance of Sunday

I had an idea that would have made everything all right.
I outlined a case that was 'screamingly funny'.
No chance of Sunday, I'm afraid. But wait, there may be.

I'll never forget my face when I came home unexpectedly.
Little imitation things were spread out on the floor.
I had an idea that would have made everything all right.

Supposing something bad happened and I had to be
      unhappy?
Old people advised me to cup my hands like this.
No chance of Sunday, I'm afraid. But wait, there may be.

I was working on a plan to do a violence to somebody.
Peculiar stuff oozed from a crack in the wall.
I had an idea that would have made everything all right,

but my room barred entrance on itself. A piece of carpet
was jammed underneath the door. I forced it with my knee.
No chance of Sunday, I'm afraid. But wait, there may be.

When you lose someone at night you have to go back
      to bed.
I'd like to wake up, but I don't really want to now.
I had an idea that would have made everything all right.
No chance of Sunday, I'm afraid. But wait, there may be.

A Boiled Egg

I lie in bed as long as possible,
having eaten my breakfast the night before.
I scribble something on my blanket
with an index finger,
then cross it out again.
Heat stands guard,
in case I try to make a break for it.

It's summer and the flesh hangs
heavy on the bone.
Cars heave themselves forward
over traffic humps, like canoes.
The rush hour comes and goes.

Is there any other breakfast
than porridge, cereal, or toast
with a boiled egg?
If you've had one of them the night before
and run out of something,
it isn't the same, you can't think straight.

I tried to imagine a kind of breakfast
made of oatmeal, sugar and milk
that wasn't porridge.
If I have a bath and wash my hair,
can I go to bed with you for two hours?
I promise to sleep all the time.

The Perfect Word

I thought of the perfect word
to describe your way of leaving,
how you performed the trick
of opening a door
and making yourself
pass through it into the street.

The word recalled exactly
how a piece of wood on a hinge
passed through an angle
of forty-five degrees,
then closed again behind you,
showing you not there.

My Letters

My letters fall behind the door.
They would like to be torn open by you.
They would like to be studied over breakfast,
sticky with marmalade.
They would like to be thrown on the fire.

My letters would like to be held in your hands,
but they don't know where you are.
They are poor blind things.
They feel around for you in the dark.
They recognise your perfume.

Black Samurai

Enter the Black Samurai,
wielding a Samurai sword,
uttering Samurai cries.
In a single circular exercise
he opens a window
in the front of your skull.
You glimpse, through crimson rain,
a loved expression,
a smile that closes up one eye.
As darkness descends,
it all comes back to you –
her face, her voice, her skin.
You taste on your tongue
the horror of lost joy.

All the Way Down

That he was still alive
all the way down,
wearing the same blue shirt,
that his wallet was
sticking out of his pocket
containing his driving licence,
saying who he was
(or who he used to be).

That he was still breathing normally
all the way down,
the expression on his face
almost unchanged,
thinking to himself:
perhaps it isn't too late
to make a new start,
really mean it this time.

The Cry

I was uttering a low cry, like a low hum or purr.
I didn't think I was crying.
I thought I had gone upstairs and was lying down.
The cry escaped me, all the time,
from where I was, in my room.
I wondered what it was for.

I looked into the cry, like looking into a box.
I thought perhaps I was suffering
and wouldn't be able to go out.
When I picked up the phone,
my mouth opened too late – the cry
was forming like a bubble at my lips.

I thought it would stop
if I thought about something else,
but I didn't know where you were. I ran outside
and saw my face at the window.
My tongue was sticking out,
I couldn't understand what I meant.

I didn't want to cry,
but I didn't want not to cry.
I waited behind the door in case I felt unhappy.
I thought it would interest me
to hear the cry crying, the room
filling up with the cry, like people making a noise.

As far as I knew I felt nothing,
only the cry vibrating like a wire
at the back of my throat, a single drawn-out note

I failed to recognise. I listened to it
getting closer, vibrating in my ears.
I thought perhaps it was yours.

Unwanted

How close to feeling ill
this ability to recall
with pinpoint accuracy
and infinite remorse
her sense of etiquette
her looking serious.

How close to death
this ability to concentrate
all night long if need be
on a single unwanted memory
the left side of her face
as she lay beside me.

I Can See Clearly Now

I have given her a mild sedation
of limeflowers and valerian.
Her breath comes easily. Her eyelids flutter.

A tune I recognise is playing in the background.
I can see clearly now.
I can see all obstacles in my way.

I pull up the covers
and tuck in her side of the bed.
It is Sunday tomorrow. No need to get up early.

Separation

Because we are able to get used to
the idea of dying, because we are able to tolerate
the suffering of loved ones,

because we are able to accustom ourselves
to every imaginable horror
without losing our appetite,

we are able to come to terms with
the idea of separation
without killing ourselves.

It hovers before our eyes,
like blood smeared down a window pane,
colouring our vision, allowing us to stay alive.

Tangles

I have been practising stroking your hair
the way you like it,
not running my fingers through it
and getting caught in all the tangles,
just rubbing lightly over your head
the way your mother used to do it,
without ever getting tired.

I have been sitting here for so long,
practising stroking your hair,
I have almost got the hang of it by now.
I do it the way you taught me,
not too hard and not too soft.
I think you would be proud
to see the progress I've made.

A Postcard

One glimpse of her handwriting
and a door clicks open in my head,
the hook of her voice
draws me upwards,
winding me in
till I can almost see her
leaning over me,
letting fall from her shoulder
something flimsy and loose.
She is blowing me kisses
from a bar in Salamanca –
'Having a brilliant time
wandering through the colourful streets
practising our Spanish.'

Last Things

I stand on a little rise
watching the long grasses swaying.
Chaos rules over there
where the last things are.
I scan the horizon,
scenting them on the wind.

A drone starts up in my head
as of insects nesting.
In the lull before the storm
last things hang back.
They jostle one another,
getting ready to be born.

When the wind changes direction
they have no choice but to happen.
Now one of them breaks cover,
makes a sudden dash.
Will it be my last swim?
Or my last Greta Garbo film?

A Game of Cards

They can't be more than nineteen or twenty,
this couple playing cards on a train,
but already he understands
that she likes being accused of cheating
when she wins all the time.
She smiles to herself as he complains.
The cards flutter through her hands
like excited tumbler pigeons.

In a break, he unfolds a newspaper
and attempts the Quick Crossword.
'What's another word for autumn?' he asks.
She is more interested in a herd of deer
grazing at the edge of a forest.
She pulls his sleeve, but it is too late.

While she's away getting drinks and snacks
he practises shuffling on his own.
The cards splutter across the table
like a burst water-main.
How happy they are, this couple on a train,
looking through holiday brochures together,
eating crisps and sharing a beer
as their life hurtles towards them.

Trains Pull Away Slowly

Sometimes you see things the way
they used to be – clouds of white smoke
standing over power stations,
washing blowing in the wind,
a bike thrown down. Poplar trees hark back
to third-class carriages
with leather window straps
and periscopes in guard's vans.

Now all the houses have a seaside look
with giant purple weeds.
The sun is going down behind a shed,
leaving a vapour trail in salmon pink.
Hay bales are small and square
the way they used to be.
Trains pull away slowly,
leaving one or two people on the platform.

The Low Branch

Freewheeling downhill
with a list in my pocket
and sun in my eyes,
I ducked my head under a low branch,
leaves brushed my face.
I was standing on the pedals,
trying to see over a wall,
when I heard the woodpecker.
I put my feet down
and waited for a moment in the shade.
There it was again –
that peal of nervous laughter,
then a flash of green
disappearing into green.

A Brass Ring

(Jardin du Luxembourg)

to Silver Eliot

The children break free from their guardians
and race one another across the park,
shouting and pointing to the little merry-go-round
lost among the chestnut trees.
Coming suddenly up close,
they stand and stare at so much terrifying fun
towering above them.
A ground-swirl of leaves eddies underfoot.

The horses are painted with cheerful names,
Bijou, Felix, Papillon, Charlot.
The lions, black Brutus and red Sultan,
drool at the heels of a camel
that nobody wants to ride because of his humps.
The man who sells tickets
helps the younger children spear the brass rings
that give free rides.

One of the stags, Rapide or Pied Leger,
looks too tired to go another step,
but somehow he carries on,
goaded to fresh efforts by his latest mistress,
severely upright in her first blue coat.
Now all the animals have a hungry look
as they chase one another
round the little wobbly track.

Something about the Moon
for Murphy

'Jeanne was dreaming,' said my daughter,
throwing back her shoulders to gain time.
She is learning Victor Hugo's poem 'Je Veux Ça'
for tomorrow morning. Line by line
she finds out how much she knows.

'Tell me what it is you desire, little Jeanne,
for I always obey these charming young women,
I lie in wait for them and I try to understand
what goes on in those divine hearts.
"I want that," said Jeanne,
pointing her finger at the sky . . .'

My daughter strides about the room,
looking for inspiration in the palm of her hand.
'It was the hour . . . It was the hour . . .
Something about the moon springing up.
O Dad, I'll never get it right.
Can I say it again from the beginning?'

I Know the Place

Hello old back bedroom where I used to work!
I was going to say 'Welcome home',
but you haven't been anywhere, have you.
It's me who's been away.
I wonder will I ever come back and start again.
My typewriter's on double spacing,
so I must have been writing prose.
Here's my stash of quarto typing paper,
my pending tray and postcard rack.
But where's my Parker 51
that left the house on pain of death?
Dear room, don't tell me you're tired too?
You look terrible! My poor old desk
has seen better days, its battered red leather
is scratched and scarred to a sort of map.
I seem to know the place.

My News

Now that the sun has made it over the tops
of the opposite houses,
flaring through the wrecks
of wallflowers and marguerites,
the seeds from giant purple flowers
spiral up over the graves
of the chrysanthemums,
one-winged sycamore planes
revolve on their axes
down through the air.

A slight breeze knocks the bell heather.
Sun wobbles in the bird mirror.
The green shed is humming.
The bare red twigs
on the upper branches of the peach tree
flick on as an electric charge hits them.
Rose brambles glisten.
The telephone wires
shoot parallel silver bullets into the blue.
How are things with you?

Sunlight Visible

Whenever I bring to mind
the folding of sheets,
the standing apart
in the morning bedroom,
the folding in two, then four –
a couple of tugs
to get all the wrinkles out –
then the bringing together
of the gathered corners,
the handing over of the sheet
to the one who must put it away,
the smell of fresh linen
rises like a benediction –
sunlight visible
in the kicked-up dust.

Gossamer Green

I see the house we didn't buy
is up for sale again.
Antique White has replaced
the London and Manchester's
trademark Gossamer Green.
The basement area has been given
a continental look,
with palm trees in earthenware pots.
A gingko guards the street.

The house we nearly bought
looks bigger now
with its roof extension and dinky balcony.
The end-of-terrace foundry
is a double garage.
The clothworkers' almshouses
are luxury maisonettes.
The house we nearly bought
has gone up in the world.

We turned our backs for a moment
and the house we didn't buy
is cashing in its chips.
What was it about the place
that made us choose the other one
round the corner,
where the school laps our front doorstep
and 'TERRY LOVES LORRAINE'
is scratched across a wall?

Three-Legged Race

Hobbled with a handkerchief, out of step,
heaving off in opposite directions,
pulling each other down,

it's obvious to anyone looking on
this isn't their event, never could be,
and yet they feel inclined to take it seriously.

Arms round one another's shoulders,
necks stretched out in concentration,
they take a few steps in unison,

before losing it again. They pick themselves up
and hurl themselves forward once more
in the general direction of the finishing line.

You can tell from the expressions on their faces
just how close they think they are
to getting the hang of it at last.

The Time of Our Lives

The future can go and be
bloody terrifying on its own
for all I care. Me and my girl
are stepping out for the past.
We're putting our best foot
backwards, heading for home.
What we'll do when we get there
we haven't decided yet.
For the time being at least
we're having the time of our lives
all over again.

Memory Dogs

When I put on my coat they're all over me
to take them up on the downs
for games with sticks.
Their eyes follow me round the room.
When I reach for a book
they hang their heads in shame.

I took them to the outskirts of town
and opened the car door.
By the time I reached home
they were waiting on the doorstep for me.
Whatever made me think
I could live without them?